Black like Me

Tracey Conley Bray

Black like Me

List of Contents

Why He Doesn't Step Up

↑

Black man we hear your plight too
many directional arrows all
intended to keep you moving
around in circles; going nowhere
fast on a collision course with
inept, failure, defeat and death.

> *Trying to rise up in a*
> *system that has*
> *systematically from your*
> *conception has placed its*
> *symbolic foot upon your*
> *neck to keep you down.*

The plan designed by the "man"
but orchestrated by the woman.
You see my young black men you

have not been the only victim of this systematic plan the black woman has also been a target of this systematic plan.

Sadly, she has been taught to fear you, to humiliate you, to walk ahead of you all under the disguise that you are not needed that your role is minimal and that it is you black man, her king and her rock, that is holding her back.

During slavery black men were sold off to destroy the black family if you cut off the head the body will eventually die off; used and abused daily made to feel like a boy even in your own home and some wonder what has taken you so long to grow up my brothers.

Truth, be told, you have been struggling and continue to struggle to stand tall on your own two feet.

Even while shinning the shoes of the feet of those that have set out to defeat you.

My black man you are no stranger to hard work "You picked cotton by day and plowed fields by night…" Black man you are intellectual beyond comparison your ideas and innovations are limitless.

You smile and bow just to stay two steps ahead so that you can protect and instill in your family the goodness of God's will.

Black man your body is hard and chiseled, black like the iron coal from the earth, you are a magnificent creation a masterpiece wonderfully made.

It is no wonder that you are feared throughout the world, not because, you are salvaged or damaged but because you was chosen for greatness.

There is no need for you to step up my black king; just assume your natural God-given role as head of your kingdom.

Then watch how all those under your kingship will strive and grow when you come to recognize the king that you are.

Broken

My life is a series of fabricated lies
woven, sewn, stitched and stringed
together much like a quilt until the
lies become my truths. You see
fear of your judgment keep my
lips seal no plans to reveal that my
story is not my own but a parody
of lies that I have chosen to own.

> **Hush child, my old
> granny would say, we are
> not the sort of people that
> hang their dirty laundry
> out for other folks to see.**

Can't you see what they are doing
to me; can't you see what this is
doing to me. You see fear of your
judgment keep my lips seal no
plans to reveal that my story is not

my own but a parody of lies that I
have chosen to own.

> **Hush child, my granny
> says to me, what happen
> in this house stays in this
> house.**

Broken I refuse to remain of two
minds to keep my sanity I rewrite
the fabric of my life every day
more fabricated lies to cover the
ones that I told on yesterday.

You see I am broken and no
amount of Elmore glue can fix me
or put me back together again, so
I piece the stories together piece
by piece, lie after lie until I have
woven together a story plot that I
can live with.

Broken and yet I still bleed why couldn't you see what this is doing to me

Hush child no more I am breaking my vow of silence, I am airing out my dirty laundry, I am telling my life story-my way so that I will finally be broken no more.

Why She Can't Step Down

Black woman you work tireless
and too many times you take care
of home all alone; with the black
man being sold off from his family
you have had to assume many
roles.

Some of these have toughen and
tested your very soul. Still you
cannot rest there are children to
be fed, homes to be kept and
work to be done.

You look around and your helpmate is gone. Just know it was designed this way to keep you from your king because a house divided against itself will surely fall.

The picture that the media and magazines paint of your king is dismal and bleak. Even when he is in the home he often, find himself fighting to find his own position.

Too often, my sister you think it is only the black man who has been victimize by this cleverly designed plan, let me caution you against this way of thinking.

Do not judge him too harshly, but do hold him accountable and while you are at it cut yourself some slack too.

You have been fed so much negative information about the black man until you unconsciously begin to internalize it, you become one of the key players in the "man" plan.

Your actions and your words convey to your displaced king that while wanted he is not needed that you got this.

He begins to feel as if he is on the auction block once again being sold to the highest bidder.

Is there work to be done between black man and woman, certainly, but this work cannot begin to take place and grow roots until we become fully cognizant of our role in the systemically designed plan to keep not only the black man but the black race down.

My sisters I beseech you instead of waiting on your king to step up and assume his rightful position;

Can you prepare the platform for him by stepping down; getting off of the throne and making room for him to sit on his throne in his own home?

In any kingdom there can exist only one king will it be him or you.

Black like Me

You say because I choose to wear my hair straight that I am trying to be European forgetting that I am a queen.

You say because I choose to paint my eyelids with all of the colors of the rainbow that I do not know who I am any more.

You say because I choose to speak the King's English that I do not know my own rich history.

That is what you say but I say I am a strong and proud black woman of African descent the daughter of former kings and queens for you see:

Many countries where built on the backs of black like me I often wonder why my blackness is so feared is it because others can see the greatness in my black skin.

> **For you see, black like me is more than big afros, full lips, wide hips, thick thighs and big behinds.**

Black man while we hold you in high esteem and recognize you as king we need for you to stand beside us, to stand up for us, to see us for more than just our physical attributes for you see:

> **The strength of a black woman character doesn't lie in her lips.**

The beautifulness of her body isn't limited to her hip.

Her aspiration and dreams aren't tied to her thighs.

Her love and patience isn't defined by her behind.

Her wisdom and knowledge flows beyond her hair designed.

For you see black like me doesn't crack under pressure or time.

Her lips, her full lips are worth more than a potter's lot, her hips were designed to create future kings and queens, in her thick thighs lies the strength to birth an entire nation of people.

Her future lies ahead of her because of the fortitude and strength left behind by those that came before her and not because of some asymmetrical behind that you deem fat…P-H-A-T

Black woman your hair is your crown and how you choose to adorn it does not define who you are for you are more than your hair and physical attributes:

> *You are doctors and lawyers, teachers and scholars, electricians and plumbers, entrepreneurial and poets, singers and dancers;*

For you see:

*Black like me birth an
entire nation of people
and black woman you are
phenomenal.*

Dysfunctional Children

C

Black man, black woman the world would have you to believe that our children are wild and untamed that they deserved to be locked up or put down permanently to protect the "man" and his family from their wild and salvage ways.

Your children "...hired by day and hunted by night..." They are the new sport, the new animals in the wild and hunting season has begun.

Our children learn early on their place in society and in the home. They too are use as instruments in the "man" plan to divide the black household.

Systemically speaking our children are used as pawns to hold us at bay; ever fearful that they will end up a victim of society ills.

Therefore, we hold on to tight or not tight enough and our message is lost and tangled up on our youths that they are important, that their lives matter and they have a right to pursue what they feel to be fundamentally right for them.

How are we expecting our black male sons to rise up and become men when the only man in the home is the woman.

Conversely, how do we expect our black female daughters to know when to step down when all she sees is a woman on the rise, consistently leading her household.

The world cries out in unison that our children are broken, incomplete and inferior to their own. When in fact their children are plagued with much of the same dysfunctions as ours.

The plan is in full force our attention have been diverted instead of instilling the good family values like those who came before us did before us so many years ago, we have succumbed we work and toil to provide material things for them to no end.

However, we have not given them the tools that they will need to survive this long hunting season that we are still in.

We have not equipped them with the voice to rise up; instead we have fallen victim to the systemically, designed plan and our children are more concerned with bling, bling than with building up.

But all is not lost once you recognize your role in the plan you can begin to implement corrective steps that will not only raise up your children but the children of your neighbors as well.

Let each one assume the natural role and responsibility bestowed upon him or her let us break this vicious curse that has our children running amuck.

If our ancestor could instill hope and raise children with good family value with the taunt of a whip or noose lingering over them.

Surely, even in this deadly and cold haunting season we too must find a way to reach our children;

atlas they will continue to see themselves through the eyes of the media and they will never be fully complete and whole.

Chasing Pipe Dreams

Life like that proverbial crack pipe that is all to precept can leave you strung out and hungry for more; always chasing after that all too familiar but unattainable and ever changing and elusive high.

What we give up and what we lay bare in hopes of reclaiming, recapturing that one brief moment that is etched in our brain.

That single, solitary, isolated fleeting moment that propels us to give up so much trying to duplicate life instead of just living in the moment; a vicious cycle of puff, puff give-puff give money, puff give furniture, puff give house, puff give job, puff give freedom, puff give family, puff give dream, puff give life.

All because we just to live; relive that one swift moment in time over and over; again and again puff, puff give.

No amount of running will ever lead you to your life path when you are caught up in the vicious spin cycle of puff, puff give; a victim of your own demise seeking without finding, grasping without seizing and breathing without living puff, puff give.

Life much like that infamous pipe keeps you hungry, keeps you coming back to that one life

altering moment in time;
time after time- puff, puff
give.

A New Form of Slavery

Out of the cotton fields and into the battle field using employment as a part of the systemically designed plan to keep black people poor, impoverished and in a new form of slavery.

> *From ordinary shacks to extraordinary rent prices in governmental instituted projects.*

The emancipation of black people presented us with a new set of problems that went above and beyond slavery. In the master house they knew their enemy he was almost always the one and the same. That was until the demoralization of the black man, black woman thinking process became infiltrated with lies and trickery.

Lynch proposed opposing young black males against old black males, light skin blacks against dark skin blacks, short blacks against tall blacks, males against females and vice versa as a strategy to tear down the black family structure.

The plan worked as systemically as it was designed to do for fear and distrust begin to brew among black people and where fear and distrust reside one can usually find envy and suspicion which leads to dissent among the people.

Can we conclude that someone has systematically done a number on the black race and be accurate, with all certainty and without any doubt?

From physical bonds of enslavement to mental enslavement whereby we are just free enough to be willingly to sing and dance to this same old tune infused with a new beat.

It is time as a people that we counter act this new form of slavery and come out from under what we have been spoon fed since birth and awaken our natural desires and inclinations to reclaim our

*power, our pride, our
people and our thrones.*

It is within each and every one of
us and they know it we just have
to come to believe and know it for
ourselves; if we were not kings
and queens there would be no
need for such an elaborate and
systemically designed plan to keep
an entire race of people
oppressed.

*Rise up, take your rightful
place you are king and I am
your queen.*

Get Your Paper Man

Don't think that I haven't noticed you day and night out grinding in these streets; I see you but while you are out there getting your hustle on don't get caught up for there are many eager to come up off of your flow.

He whispers from afar get your weight up stack them dollars up get your paper man.

He screams in her ear get your weight down you got to look the part get your paper man.

Come in early grind real hard but clock in on time get your paper man.

Work overtime put in extra hours but clock out on time get your paper man.

Go at it hard from dust to dawn ignore the pain in your arm get your paper man.

Forget about eating paint a picture that is equal to the Mona Lisa get your paper man.

Write a book about life; the life that you are not living sell it lies to the people get your paper man.

Give the radio DJ a free CD and your fan a free diss get your paper man

Just know that it is not personal just the cost of doing business any town, any city get your paper man.

Reflection

It is the hope of the author that this bridge book has caused you the reader to pause and reflect on how you may be unknowingly working to further the systemically designed plan to keep the black race divided so that they are easier to conquer. The author intent is not to fan the flames of racism and prejudice but to educate, inform and invite others to join her in rising up to our natural state as kings and queens.

Questions to Ponder

As a black man what are some steps that I can take to improve the black man/black woman relationship?

_____
_____
_____
_____
_____
_____
_____
_____
_____
_____
_____
_____
_____
_____
_____
_____
_____
_____
_____

As a black woman what are some steps that I can take to improve the black man/black woman relationship?

_____

_____

_____

_____

_____

_____

_____

_____

_____

_____

_____

_____

_____

_____

_____

_____

_____

_____

_____

_____

_____

_____

Why is it imperative that we mend the relationship with our black female/male counterpart

_____
_____
_____
_____
_____
_____
_____
_____
_____
_____
_____
_____
_____
_____
_____
_____
_____
_____
_____
_____
_____
_____
_____

Define the black man and his importance
in the family dynamics?

_____
_____
_____
_____
_____
_____
_____
_____
_____
_____
_____
_____
_____
_____
_____
_____
_____
_____
_____
_____
_____
_____
_____

Define the black woman and her
importance to the family dynamics?

_____

_____

_____

_____

_____

_____

_____

_____

_____

_____

_____

_____

_____

_____

_____

_____

_____

_____

_____

_____

_____

_____

_____

Letter to a King

If you could share one thing with the
black man, what would it be?

_____

_____

_____

_____

_____

_____

_____

_____

_____

_____

_____

_____

_____

_____

_____

_____

_____

_____

_____

_____

Letter to a Queen

If you could share one thing with the
black woman, what would it be?

_____

_____

_____

_____

_____

_____

_____

_____

_____

_____

_____

_____

_____

_____

_____

_____

_____

_____

_____

_____

_____

Where do we go from here, how do we
begin to repair the relationship between
the black male and female?

_____

_____

_____

_____

_____

_____

_____

_____

_____

_____

_____

_____

_____

_____

_____

_____

_____

_____

_____

_____

_____

What role, if any, did welfare and public housing play in the demise of the black man and woman relationship?

_____

_____

_____

_____

_____

_____

_____

_____

_____

_____

_____

_____

_____

_____

_____

_____

_____

_____

_____

_____

_____

_____

_____

_____

_____

How can researching about "Black Wall Street" lead the black male/female relationship in the right direction?

_____
_____
_____
_____
_____
_____
_____
_____
_____
_____
_____
_____
_____
_____
_____
_____
_____
_____
_____
_____
_____
_____

How does negative images and stereotypes affects relationships in the black community?

_____
_____
_____
_____
_____
_____
_____
_____
_____
_____
_____
_____
_____
_____
_____
_____
_____
_____
_____
_____
_____
_____

Now ask yourself, are you ready to begin
actively participating in the healing
process?

_____
_____
_____
_____
_____
_____
_____
_____
_____
_____
_____
_____
_____
_____
_____
_____
_____
_____
_____
_____
_____
_____
_____
_____